I0151566

Bonita and the Barn on Hiram Edson's Farm

by Linda May Everhart

**Illustrations by
Maksym Stasiuk**

Dedication

This book was written to honor all the volunteers who have used their skills to joyfully and sacrificially maintain and improve the Adventist Heritage sites so that Seventh-day Adventist history might be preserved.

TEACH Services, Inc.
P U B L I S H I N G
www.TEACHServices.com • (800) 367-1844

Mama, Samuel, Sara, and Sofia are so excited! They are on their way to the Hiram Edson Farm. The Hiram Edson Farm is a place where people can go to learn what God taught the Adventist people about what Jesus has been doing in heaven and what He will do when He returns to earth.

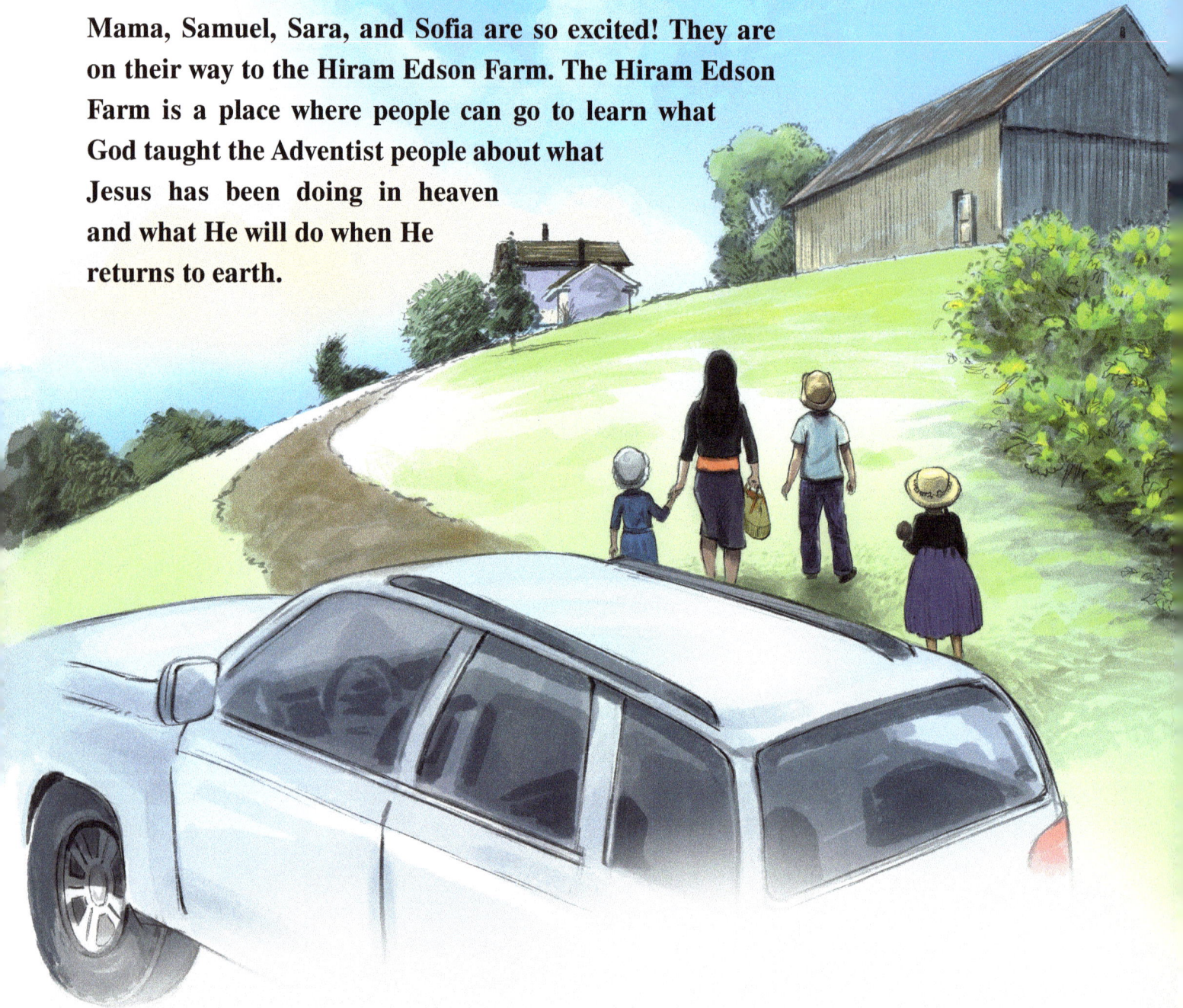

Mama parks the car, and they walk up the hill to the house and barn. Inside the house, Mama and the children see things that take them back in time.

Samuel sees a note that Hiram Edson wrote. He tries to read it, but the letters are all slanty and connected. He smiles when he notices that somebody has copied the words so he can read them.

Sara and Sofia walk over to a little table that has a colorful tent on it surrounded by little wooden objects. Mama is right behind.

"Mama, what's that?"

"That's the sanctuary from the Old Testament. God had the children of Israel build it so they could understand what God would do to save people from their sins. It symbolizes Jesus' death and what He is doing up in heaven right now."

Sara finds a nice little bench by the window and sits down with her doll, Bonita, to enjoy the sunshine peeking through the window. She turns her head to notice a little pump organ and thinks, *Wouldn't it be nice to play it!*

Just then, a lady in a long, dark dress walks over to the organ and looks at Sara.

"Would you like to see how it works?"

Sara nods her head. The lady opens up a little songbook and puts it on the organ. Then she sits down and starts pumping the organ's pedals as she plays and sings:

"You will see your Lord a-comin', you will see your Lord a-comin'. You will see your Lord a-comin' in a few more days...."

As the lady sings and plays, Sara smiles and looks down at Bonita. She is just a doll, but Sara likes to pretend that she can see what's going on and that she is enjoying the music, too.

Mama calls for Sara, Samuel, and Sofia to go outside and enjoy the farm.

Outside are apple, pear, cherry, and peach trees. There are berry vines, too. Sofia pricks her finger while picking a raspberry.

"Ouch!"

Mama kisses her boo boo and tells her, "When Jesus comes and makes the world again, there won't be any thorns to hurt our fingers."

Samuel spies a trail that curves through a flower garden into some trees beyond. One of the heritage volunteers tells them that people take the trail to pray and learn about God through paintings and stories written along the way.

They feel the warm sun on their skin, they hear the happy song of the birds in the trees, and they smell the sweet perfume of the flowers in the air. What a pleasant day!

The first painting posted along the trail is of people rising up into the air, looking, with happy faces, at Jesus who is coming with all His angels in the clouds. Sara notices something special.

"Mama, look! That angel is handing a little girl to her mommy and daddy."

"That's right, Sara. The little girl's parents were once very sad when their little girl died. But look how happy they are now!"

They come to another picture. Samuel is curious.

"Why are those angels in the picture chasing the other angels, Mama?"

Mama reads a verse posted by the painting:

"And war broke out in heaven: Michael and his angels
fought with the dragon; and the dragon and his
angels fought, but they did not prevail, nor
was a place found for them in heaven any
longer." (Revelation 12:7, 8, NKJV)

Mama explains:

"An angel named Lucifer told the other angels lies about the Heavenly Father. He said that God did not really love them. Some of the angels believed the lie; most did not. Then war broke out in heaven and Satan and his angels had to leave! They took their lies to earth and Lucifer, now called Satan, got Adam and Eve to distrust God too.

"Though the angels were really sad that some of their angel friends had to leave heaven and that Adam and Eve joined Satan in not trusting God's love, God had a plan to save human beings. He would send His Son Jesus to be born into this world, and, even though a jealous king would try to kill Him, Jesus would escape to carry out God's plan."

Sara sits down on a bench beside the path and thinks about Jesus as a baby. She smiles as she hugs her dolly Bonita.

The next painting along the path is of Jesus on the cross. It makes everybody sad to see Jesus suffering, but Mama says,

"Remember, even though Jesus died for our sins, He rose from the dead to tell His disciples the good news before He went back to heaven. Because of His death, we can be forgiven and He will come back in the clouds to take us home with Him."

At last the family comes to a painting of Hiram Edson. He is standing in a cornfield, looking up at something in the sky that looks like the tent temple they saw in the house. In the tent, Jesus is dressed in the clothes of the priest.

Mama reads the sign beside the painting and tells the children,

"This sign tell about what led Hiram Edson and others to read the Bible. They found out about a time when Jesus, the High Priest, started looking into records to decide who would be happy to be in heaven with Him. That time started in 1844 and is still going on now. It is good news to those who are God's friends!"

In another painting, angels are shown warning people to be ready when Jesus comes. Mama reads the sign beside the picture and then turns to her three children,

"This picture teaches that those who will be happy to see Jesus come are trusting in God and keeping God's Ten Commandments.

"Those who go up into the clouds with Jesus will get to drink from the crystal-clear stream and eat from the tree of life in the new Jerusalem. Even better, they will get to see and walk with Jesus. In heaven and on the new earth, no animal will bite anybody or any other animal. And no one will ever get hurt or sick again."

Mama, Samuel, Sara, and Sofia now walk quietly over to Hiram Edson's barn. Each is thinking about what they have just seen.

It is almost time to leave. Mama says, "Children, before our long ride home, why don't you go outside and play for a while." Sara puts Bonita on top of an old barrel in the barn and smiles as she thinks how comfortable her doll looks there.

Before long, dark clouds fill the skies, and Mama calls out,

"Hurry, children, we've got to go!"

All three children obey their mother and run to the car.

The lighting flashes and the thunder goes, "Ka-boom!" Rain is coming down hard, as they drive away, and the windshield wiper can hardly keep the front window clear. The children look forward with big open eyes as Mama goes slowly down the road. Suddenly Sara remembers her doll.

"Mama! I left Bonita in the barn. Can't we go back and get her?"

"I'm sorry, sweetie, but the storm is too bad. We have to get back home. We can drive back to the barn tomorrow."

Thinking of Bonita being left all alone makes Sara very, very sad. But she knows Mama is right and that they will go back as she promised.

During worship at home, Mama tells them more about Hiram Edson and about how he was left in his barn, praying through his tears when Jesus didn't come. Yet, Hiram Edson remembered Jesus' promise:

> "Let not your heart be troubled; you believe in God, believe also in Me. In My Father's house are many mansions; if it were not so, I would have told you. I go to prepare a place for you. And if I go and prepare a place for you, I will come again and receive you to Myself; that where I am, there you may be also." (John 14:1–3, NKJV)

They kneel for prayer and Mama thanks Jesus for keeping them safe in the storm. She also prays that they can all get a good night's sleep.

Sara is worried about her little doll and imagines a little gray mouse sniffing Bonita to see if she is something to eat. However, trusting that Jesus will take care of Bonita until they get back, she also imagines a hungry barn owl coming to Bonita's rescue.

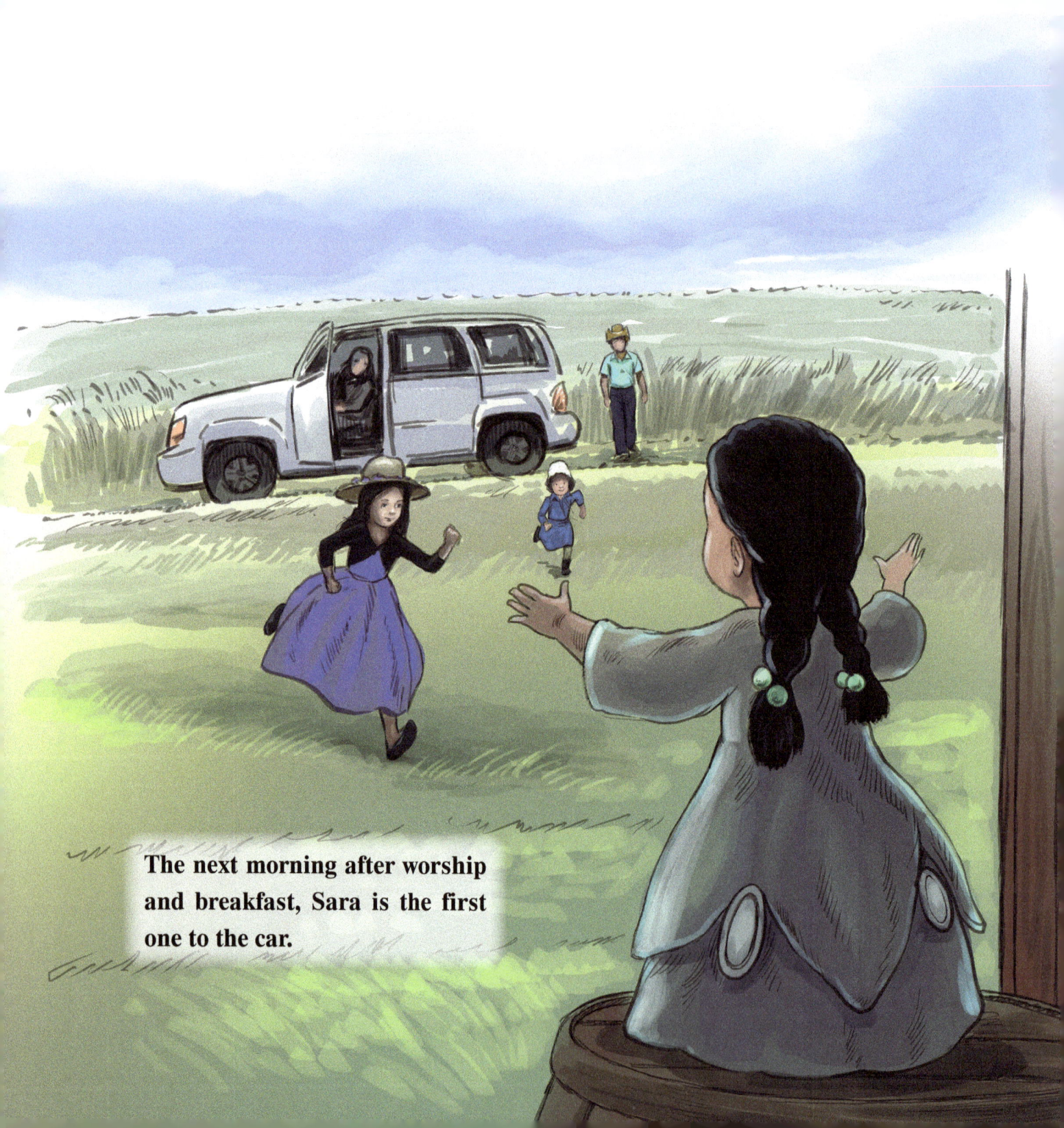

The next morning after worship and breakfast, Sara is the first one to the car.

When they get to the Hiram Edson farm, she rushes to the barn and finds Bonita still on top of the barrel. Sara picks up her doll and hugs her tight.

Mama and the other children catch up, and Mama says,

"Let's thank God for taking care of Bonita."

Sara prays: "Dear Father in heaven, thank you that nothing bad happened to Bonita and that you answered our prayers. Help me never to forget Bonita again. In Jesus' name I pray, Amen."

Samuel says, "Amen!"

After one last look at the farm, Mama and the children start singing the song they learned just the day before:

> "You will see your Lord a-comin',
> You will see your Lord a-comin',
> You will see your Lord a-comin' in a few more days...."

Excitedly Sara breaks in.

"Mama, Mama, I've just thought of something special about Jesus. He really wants to come back to earth and get us—just like I really wanted to go back to the farm and get Bonita!"

"Yes, Sara, and Jesus wants to get us even *more* than you wanted to get Bonita."

Sara looks off into the sky with a big smile, and Samuel starts the song up again, as Mama and Sofia join in.

NOTES

This book helps make the story of the early advent believers in Hiram Edson's time relevant for children. Those who waited for Jesus to return on October 22, 1844, weathered their storm of disappointment because they, like William Miller, could say, "In Jesus I found a Friend." Trusting our heavenly Friend when we don't understand the events we are experiencing develops a faith in us that God will take care of us through the uncertainty that is yet to come.

This story was written to help children understand the feelings of uncertainty and abandonment that the early advent believers went through. Hiram Edson explained how he felt:

> I mused in my heart, saying, my advent experience has been the richest and brightest of all my Christian experience. If this had proved a failure, what was the rest of my Christian experience worth? Has the Bible proved a failure? Is there no God,—no heaven,—no golden home city,—no paradise? Is all this but a cunningly devised fable? Is there no reality to our fondest hopes and expectations of these things? (James R. Nix, *The Life and Work of Hiram Edson*, p. 9)

When Edson later grasped the bigger picture of what Jesus is now doing in preparation for His second coming, there was an explosion of understanding that made him want to share the good news of the gospel and of Jesus' return.

The role of this book is to explain the disappointment of the early pioneers and their renewal of faith and love for the One who loves us and longs to have us with Him forever.

www.ingramcontent.com/pod-product-compliance
Lightning Source LLC
Chambersburg PA
CBHW061416090426

42742CB00026B/3486